The Lender-Placed Flood Insurance Market for Residential Properties

Lloyd Dixon, Noreen Clancy,
Bruce Bender, Patricia K. Ehrler

Prepared for the Mitigation Division of
the Federal Emergency Management Agency

Approved for public release; distribution unlimited

INFRASTRUCTURE, SAFETY, AND ENVIRONMENT and
INSTITUTE FOR CIVIL JUSTICE

The research described in this report was sponsored by the Mitigation Division of the Federal Emergency Management Agency under contract number HSFEHQ-04-F-0431.

Library of Congress Cataloging-in-Publication Data

978-0-8330-4155-5

The RAND Corporation is a nonprofit research organization providing objective analysis and effective solutions that address the challenges facing the public and private sectors around the world. RAND's publications do not necessarily reflect the opinions of its research clients and sponsors.

RAND® is a registered trademark.

Published 2007 by the RAND Corporation
1776 Main Street, P.O. Box 2138, Santa Monica, CA 90407-2138
1200 South Hayes Street, Arlington, VA 22202-5050
4570 Fifth Avenue, Pittsburgh, PA 15213-2665
RAND URL: http://www.rand.org/
To order RAND documents or to obtain additional information, contact
Distribution Services: Telephone: (310) 451-7002;
Fax: (310) 451-6915; Email: order@rand.org

Preface

The National Flood Insurance Program (NFIP), which is run by the Federal Emergency Management Agency (FEMA), provides the majority of flood insurance on residential properties in the United States. While insurance agents sell nearly all NFIP policies through private insurance companies, NFIP policies are still underwritten by the federal government. Flood insurance is also available from private insurers that assume the risk of losses themselves. Little systematic information is available, however, about the size of the private market, how the policies offered by private insurers compare with those offered by the NFIP, and the reasons buyers choose private market policies over federal program policies.

This report attempts to more precisely quantify private insurers' role in underwriting flood insurance on residential structures and condominium units, focusing on policies placed by lenders to comply with the NFIP's mandatory purchase requirement (MPR). This information will help FEMA staff more fully understand and quantify the percentage of homes financially protected by flood insurance. This report also analyzes how lender-placed flood insurance policies compare with those offered by the NFIP and examines the structure and buyer perceptions of the private market. This information will help FEMA staff assess the extent to which such private policies meet the MPR's insurance standards and help Congress, FEMA, and other stakeholders develop and evaluate proposals to improve the public and private mechanisms in place to provide insurance against flood risk.

Related work at RAND on flood insurance and compensation and insurance for disasters more generally include

- *The National Flood Insurance Program's Market Penetration Rate: Estimates and Policy Implications*, Lloyd Dixon, Noreen Clancy, Seth A. Seabury, Adrian Overton, TR-300-FEMA, 2006
- *Distribution of Losses from Large Terrorist Attacks Under the Terrorism Risk Insurance Act*, Stephen J. Carroll, Tom LaTourrette, Brian G. Chow, Gregory S. Jones, Craig Martin, MG-427-CTRMP, 2005
- *Issues and Options for Government Intervention in the Market for Terrorism Insurance*, Lloyd Dixon, John Arlington, Stephen Carroll, Darius Lakdawalla, Robert Reville, David Adamson, OP-135-ICJ, 2004
- *Compensation for Losses from the 9/11 Attacks*, Lloyd Dixon and Rachel Kaganoff Stern, MG-264-ICJ, 2004.

This research was sponsored by the Mitigation Division of FEMA. Authors Lloyd Dixon and Noreen Clancy are at RAND; Bruce Bender heads Bender Consulting Services of Scottsdale, Arizona; and Patricia K. Ehrler contributed to this project as a consultant based in Austin, Texas. For more information about this study, contact

Lloyd Dixon
RAND Corporation
1776 Main Street
P.O. Box 2138
Santa Monica, CA 90407-2138
310-393-0411 x7480
Lloyd_Dixon@rand.org

RAND Infrastructure, Safety, and Environment and the RAND Institute for Civil Justice

This research was conducted as a joint effort of the Environment, Energy, and Economic Development Program (EEED) within RAND Infrastructure, Safety, and Environment (ISE) and of the RAND Institute for Civil Justice (ICJ).

The mission of ISE is to improve the development, operation, use, and protection of society's essential physical assets and natural resources and to enhance the related social assets of safety and security of individuals in transit and in their workplaces and communities. The EEED research portfolio addresses environmental quality and regulation, energy resources and systems, water resources and systems, climate, natural hazards and disasters, and economic development—both domestically and internationally. EEED research is conducted for government, foundations, and the private sector.

ICJ is an independent research program within the RAND Corporation. The mission of ICJ, a division of the RAND Corporation, is to improve private and public decisionmaking on civil legal issues by supplying policymakers and the public with the results of objective, empirically based, analytic research. ICJ facilitates change in the civil justice system by analyzing trends and outcomes, identifying and evaluating policy options, and bringing together representatives of different interests to debate alternative solutions to policy problems. ICJ builds on a long tradition of RAND research characterized by an interdisciplinary, empirical approach to public policy issues and rigorous standards of quality, objectivity, and independence.

All RAND research products are subject to peer review before publication. RAND publications do not necessarily reflect the opinions or policies of the research sponsors, the ICJ Board of Overseers, or the ISE Advisory Board.

Information about ICJ is available online (http://www.rand.org/icj). Inquiries about ICJ research projects should be sent to the following address:

Robert T. Reville, Director
RAND Institute for Civil Justice

1776 Main Street
P.O. Box 2138
Santa Monica, CA 90407-2138
310-393-0411 x6786
Fax: 310-451-6979
Robert_Reville@rand.org

Information about EEED is also available online (http://www.rand.org/ise/environ).
Inquiries about EEED projects should be sent to the following address:

Michael Toman, Director
Environment, Energy, and Economic Development Program, ISE
RAND Corporation
1200 South Hayes Street
Arlington, VA 22202-5050
703-413-1100, x5189
Michael_Toman@rand.org

Contents

Figures

Tables

Summary

The National Flood Insurance Program (NFIP) provides the majority of flood insurance on residential properties in the United States.[1] While insurance agents sell nearly all NFIP policies through private insurance companies, NFIP policies are still underwritten by the federal government. Flood insurance is also available from private insurers that assume the risk of losses themselves. However, little systematic information is available about the size of the private market, how the policies offered by private insurers compare with those offered by the NFIP, or the reasons buyers choose private market policies over federal program policies. This report provides information in each of these three areas.

Overview of the Private Market for Residential Flood Insurance

Established by Congress in 1968, the NFIP makes flood insurance available to homeowners, renters, and businesses in communities that participate in the NFIP. Such communities agree to adopt and enforce a floodplain management program aimed at reducing flood losses. Early in the program, the federal government found that making insurance available was not sufficient to induce large numbers of people to purchase flood insurance, and, in the Flood Disaster Protection Act of 1973, Congress established the mandatory purchase requirement (MPR). The MPR requires homeowners in areas at high flood risk to purchase flood insurance if they have a mortgage with a federally regulated lender. Lenders must ensure that the property is covered by flood insurance for the term of the loan and are required to purchase flood insurance on behalf of the property owner if the property owner fails to do so.

Private insurers provide flood insurance through the voluntary and the lender-placed markets. In the voluntary market, homeowners choose whether to purchase flood insurance underwritten by private insurers or the NFIP. Only a few private insurers offer policies in the voluntary market, and the number of policies written outside the NFIP remains very small. In 1991, the NFIP introduced a special program to enable lenders to more easily force-place policies: the Mortgage Portfolio Protection Program (MPPP). However, the MPPP policy is little

---

[1] The Federal Emergency Management Agency (FEMA), which is part of the U.S. Department of Homeland Security (DHS), runs the NFIP.

xiv   The Lender-Placed Flood Insurance Market for Residential Properties

used now, and, instead, lenders for the most part force-place policies that private sector insurers underwrite. This study focused on the size and characteristics of this lender-placed market.[2]

Large lenders subject to the MPR typically hire firms referred to as *trackers* to monitor whether the homes in their portfolios carry the required amounts of flood and other insurance. If a home in a high-risk flood area lacks insurance, trackers often first call to confirm whether the home has flood insurance and then send out a series of letters that culminates in the force placement of flood insurance if the homeowner fails to purchase insurance. Federal regulation requires a 45-day notice period before force-placing flood insurance.

Size of the Lender-Placed Flood Insurance Market

To develop estimates of the number of lender-placed policies that private insurers underwrite, we collected data from a sample of lenders, trackers, and insurers. While the sample sizes were not large (four insurers, four trackers, and five lenders), the insurers and trackers participating in the study represent a sizable share of the lender-placed market by policies issued and loans tracked.[3] The lenders participating in the study represent a modest share of the market by loan volume. We used methods detailed in the report to extrapolate the number of policies that participating firms reported to the industry as a whole.

As shown in Table S.1, estimates based on the different data sources are internally consistent and point to between roughly 130,000 and 190,000 private lender–placed flood insurance policies. The figures count only primary flood insurance policies—that is, policies that assume that no other flood coverage on the property. Lenders were not able to provide data on policies in place on second mortgages and home equity loans, and adjustments were made to estimate the number of such policies. Construction of quantitative measures of the statistical

Table S.1
Estimated Number of Primary Lender–Placed Flood Insurance Policies Written by Private Insurers

Source of Data Used for Estimate	Policies in Place (thousands)
Insurers	128 to 187
Lenders	
Excluding second mortgages and home equity loans	110
With adjustment to account for second mortgages and home equity loans	154
Trackers	142

NOTE: Estimates reflect policies in place some time between mid-2004 and early 2006.

---

[2] Private insurers provide flood insurance for most commercial structures and, in contrast to practices for residential structures, provide it through the voluntary market rather than the mandatory market. Investigation of the size of the flood insurance market on commercial studies was outside the scope of this study.

[3] Knowledgeable stakeholders interviewed for the project indicated that eight insurers write the vast majority of lender-placed flood insurance policies and that seven firms track the vast majority of loans tracked by the tracking industry.

uncertainty of the estimates was beyond the scope of this study, but the consistency of the estimates across the different data sources increases confidence in the findings.

Private insurers also appear to write a sizable number of gap policies, although the data on gap policies are sketchy. Gap policies add to the coverage of an existing flood insurance policy and are issued when the lender determines that there is insufficient coverage. Including gap policies may increase the number of private policies to between 180,000 and 260,000. This prediction is quite speculative, however, and further investigation of the number of gap policies is warranted. Gap policies do not increase the total number of households covered by flood insurance but rather increase the dollar amount of flood insurance in place.

The number of private policies is not large compared with the 5.0 million residential policies written by the NFIP. Including this relatively small number of private policies thus does not result in a large increase in estimates of the proportion of structures covered by flood insurance.[4] However, the number of policies currently in place is not the only measure of private insurers' importance in implementing the MPR. First, few lender-placed policies remain in effect for the one-year policy term, with the implication that far more policies are issued per year than the number of policies currently in place indicates. Second, the automatic coverage endorsement that many lenders purchased increases the number of homes effectively insured beyond the number of policies in place.[5]

Comparison of Private and NFIP Policies

Private policies used to satisfy the MPR must meet or exceed coverage provided by NFIP policies. To assess whether private policies satisfy this requirement, we compared the provisions of five private policies with the standard flood insurance policy used by the NFIP (the policy that lenders can place through the NFIP's MPPP).

The administrative features of private policies are, for the most part, broader or more flexible than those of the NFIP policy. Private insurers offer several optional endorsements and provide features such as backdating, gap policies, and automatic coverage that enhance a lender's ability to tailor the coverage to its portfolio's particular characteristics. In terms of administrative features, the only area in which private policies are more limited is the appeal of claims payments.

Private policies provide broader coverage for some risks than the NFIP policy does but provide less broad coverage for other risks. On the one hand, private policies cover mudslides, while the MPPP policy does not. On the other, some private policies have stronger mold exclusions than the NFIP policy has. In addition, the private policies reviewed do not cover testing,

---

[4] Dixon, Clancy, et al. (2006, p. 15) estimated that 1.76 million of the 3.57 million single-family homes in Special Flood Hazard Areas (SFHAs) carry policies from the NFIP (49 percent). If private lender–placed policies increase the number of single-family homes insured by 160,000, the market penetration rate for flood insurance (including both NFIP and non-NFIP policies) would rise to 54 percent.

[5] With the automatic coverage endorsement, all homes in the lender's portfolio subject to the MPR are in effect covered for losses.

monitoring, or cleanup of pollution that occurs during a flood event, while the NFIP policy covers cleanup even though it excludes coverage for testing and monitoring.

We also found that, in terms of the types of and limits on losses that private policies cover, private policies compare favorably with the NFIP policy in many dimensions, but they also come up short in a few. Areas in which the private policies reviewed meet or exceed NFIP policy provisions include

- the policy limit on structure coverage
- situations in which the policy pays replacement cost rather than actual cash value of the loss
- additional living expenses
- basement coverage.

Areas in which the provisions of some private policies were more restrictive than the NFIP policy include

- debris removal
- coverage for loss avoidance measures
- limits on increased cost of compliance coverage.

The failure to meet or exceed NFIP policies in some dimensions raises the possibility that some private policies do not comply with MPR requirements. It is up to policymakers to assess whether these differences are significant. Some of the private policies may have been updated since we obtained the policies (early to mid-2005), and additional research is warranted on the extent to which coverage in these dimensions has improved over time.

Perceptions of the Advantages of the Private Market

We interviewed lenders, insurers, and trackers about the advantages and disadvantages of force-placing policies through the private market rather than through the NFIP. We interviewed 11 firms in total, either in person or via phone.

Private policies offer a number of features attractive to lenders that NFIP policies do not. The stakeholders interviewed highlighted the ability to backdate private policies to the start of the letter cycle and the automatic coverage endorsement. They also praised the service that private insurers provided and the ease of using their products. Lenders appeared very satisfied with the products and services that private insurers provided and expressed no interest in using the MPPP to force-place policies. The MPPP would need to change in fundamental ways to attract private lenders and trackers to use it.

Role of Private Insurers

Congress established the NFIP in part due to the ongoing unavailability of private flood insurance. Over the years, however, a deepening partnership has emerged between the federal government and the private insurance industry. The primary role the private insurance industry plays in providing flood insurance to residential structures is to administer the NFIP. However, private insurers underwrite flood insurance in a limited, but important, niche. In doing so, they increase the number of homes protected by flood insurance, developing innovative policy provisions that respond to lender and borrower needs and providing streamlined services that reduce the costs lenders incur in complying with the MPR.

Acknowledgments

This report would not have been possible without the participation of insurers, lenders, and trackers that are involved in the lender-placed market for residential flood insurance. They took time out of their busy schedules to respond to our data requests and to complete telephone or in-person interviews on the structure and operation of the lender-placed flood insurance market. We thank them heartily for their efforts.

David Thomas, our project officer at FEMA, provided helpful feedback during the course of the project and comments on various interim briefings and drafts. We would also to thank the National Lender Insurance Council (NLIC), a nonprofit trade association whose mission is to reduce insurable losses through government-industry partnerships, education, and dialogue, for their help in recruiting lenders, insurers, and trackers to participate in the study. We would like in particular to acknowledge the efforts of Michael Moye, president of the NLIC, and Carolyn Irwin-Torina, vice president of the NLIC and assistant vice president at Flagstar Bank.

Seth A. Seabury at RAND and Raymond Reed at Lenpex, LLC, a firm that specializes in insurance for lenders, provided technical reviews of the draft report. Their helpful comments improved the quality of the report. Susan M. Gates coordinated the review process at RAND and Nancy Good at RAND provided assistance in assembling the document. Lisa Bernard ably edited the document, and Josh Levine did an excellent job as production editor.

Abbreviations

BFE	Base Flood Elevation
CBRA	Coastal Barrier Resource Act
DHS	U.S. Department of Homeland Security
EEED	Environment, Energy, and Economic Development
Fannie Mae	Federal National Mortgage Association
FEMA	Federal Emergency Management Agency
FIRM	flood insurance rate map
Freddie Mac	Federal Home Loan Mortgage Corporation
GSE	government-sponsored enterprise
ICJ	RAND Institute for Civil Justice
ISE	RAND Infrastructure, Safety, and Environment
MPPP	Mortgage Portfolio Protection Plan
MPR	mandatory purchase requirement
NFIP	National Flood Insurance Program
NLIC	National Lender Insurance Council
SFHA	Special Flood Hazard Area
WYO	Write Your Own

CHAPTER ONE

Introduction

The National Flood Insurance Program (NFIP) provides the majority of flood insurance on residential properties in the United States.[1] While insurance agents sell nearly all NFIP policies through private insurance companies, the federal government still underwrites them. Flood insurance is also available from private insurers that underwrite it themselves and assume the risk. However, little systematic information is available about the size of the private market, how the policies offered by private insurers compare with those offered by the NFIP, and the reasons buyers choose private market policies over federal program policies.

This report attempts to more precisely quantify the role of private insurers in underwriting flood insurance on residential structures and condominium units.[2] It focuses on private insurers' role in writing the policies that banks and other lenders place to comply with the NFIP's mandatory purchase requirement (MPR). This information will help FEMA staff more fully understand and quantify the percentage of homes that are financially protected by flood insurance and that comply with the MPR. This report also investigates how lender-placed flood insurance policies compare with those offered by the NFIP and examines the structure and buyer perceptions of the private market. This information will help FEMA staff assess the extent to which such private policies satisfy MPR coverage requirements and help Congress, FEMA, and other stakeholders develop and evaluate proposals to improve the public and private mechanisms in place to provide insurance against flood risk.

In the remainder of this chapter, we provide an overview of the NFIP, the various market segments that private flood insurers serve, and the primary actors in the market segment driven by the MPR. The chapter concludes with a preview of the remainder of the report.

---

[1] The Federal Emergency Management Agency (FEMA), which is part of the U.S. Department of Homeland Security (DHS), runs the NFIP.

[2] *Residential structures* typically refers to structures with four or fewer housing units. Structures with more than four housing units, such as apartment buildings, are considered commercial structures, as are structures that support industrial or commercial activities. Residential condominium units, even if in structures with more than four units, are often combined with residential structures in analyses of housing markets, and we follow this practice in this report.

The National Flood Insurance Program

The NFIP makes flood insurance available to homeowners, renters, and businesses in communities that participate in the NFIP. Such communities agree to adopt and enforce a floodplain management program aimed at reducing flood losses. The program's central requirement is that new residential construction in high-risk areas known as Special Flood Hazard Areas (SFHAs) be elevated to or above the level that water would reach in a flood that occurs with a 1-percent annual chance (the Base Flood Elevation, or BFE).[3] Existing residential structures that are not built at or above BFE must also be raised to BFE if they are more than 50-percent damaged by flood or 50-percent substantially improved. New nonresidential construction in the SFHA must be either elevated or floodproofed against the 1-percent annual chance flood (FEMA, 2002, p. 13).

Early in the program, the federal government found that making insurance available, even at subsidized rates for *existing* buildings, was not a sufficient incentive for communities to join the NFIP or for individuals to purchase flood insurance. In response, Congress passed the Flood Disaster Protection Act of 1973, which obligates federally regulated lenders to require flood insurance as a condition of granting or continuing a loan when the buildings and improvements securing it are in the SFHA of a community participating in the NFIP. Loans on homes in SFHAs sold to government-sponsored enterprises (GSEs) such as the Federal National Mortgage Association (Fannie Mae) and Federal Home Loan Mortgage Corporation (Freddie Mac) are also subject to this MPR.[4] The number of communities participating in the program and the number of policyholders grew dramatically as a result. Currently, more than 20,000 communities participate in the NFIP, and more than 5.2 million flood policies are in place (NFIP, undated).[5] A high percentage of NFIP policies are on residential housing units. Of the 5.2 million policies, 5.0 million are residential (defined as policies covering one- to four-unit structures plus condominium units).[6]

The NFIP offers a maximum $250,000 in structure coverage and up to $100,000 in contents coverage for residential buildings and individual condominium units.[7] Nonresidential buildings are eligible for up to $500,000 building coverage and $500,000 contents coverage (FEMA, 2002, p. 25).

---

[3] SFHAs are areas at high risk of flooding and are identified on FEMA's flood insurance rate maps (FIRMs) as having at least a 1-percent chance of flooding in any given year. The SFHA does not necessarily cover all the flood-prone areas in a community. Small, noncontiguous areas in an NFIP community that have at least a 1-percent chance of flooding, for example, are often not identified on FIRMs.

[4] The National Flood Insurance Reform Act of 1994 strengthened the MPR.

[5] There were 5.236 million policies in place as of July 31, 2006, and 4.646 million policies in place as of August 1, 2005 (prior to Hurricane Katrina).

[6] A single NFIP insurance contract can cover multiple units in a condominium building. When reporting the number of policies in force, the NFIP counts each condominium unit covered as a separate policy. In July 2006, 5.2 policies were in force and 4.3 million contracts were in force (NFIP, undated).

[7] Residential condominium buildings can purchase up to $250,000 times the number of units and up to $100,000 in commonly owned contents coverage per building (NFIP, ongoing, p. CONDO-6).

The private sector insurers that issue and service the vast majority of NFIP policies are referred to as *Write-Your-Own (WYO) Companies*.[8] These companies market flood insurance, collect the information needed to issue a policy, and adjust flood insurance claims on the policies they service.[9] The federal government retains the insurance risk for the policies. The WYO companies receive an expense allowance from the NFIP per policy written and claim adjusted and remit premium income in excess of claims to the federal government. This report does not address the role of the private sector in the operation of the NFIP. Rather, it examines the role the private sector plays in issuing and underwriting flood policies that the NFIP does not underwrite.

Overview of the Private Market for Residential Flood Insurance

Private insurers underwrite flood insurance in both the voluntary market and the lender-placed market. The lender-placed market is also referred to as the *force-placed market*. Below, we first describe the voluntary and lender-placed markets and then describe the primary actors in the lender-placed market.

Voluntarily Purchased and Lender-Placed Private Flood Insurance

A homeowner might choose to purchase a policy from the private sector rather than the NFIP to secure coverage in areas in which the NFIP policies are not available[10] or to obtain higher policy limits or broader coverage than those available from the NFIP. A few insurers offer flood insurance policies in this voluntary market. They generally target high net worth households and include flood insurance in a package that covers multiple assets and perils. Lloyd's of London syndicates have offered voluntary policies for a number of years, and large insurers such as AIG, Fireman's Fund, and Chubb have entered this market in the past few years, focusing mainly on homes in low- and moderate-risk areas (outside SFHAs).[11] Systematic information on the number of private residential policies purchased through the voluntary market is not available, but the number is thought to be small (Bender, 2006). Consequently, this report focuses on the lender-placed market, although further research on the size of the voluntary private flood insurance market is warranted.

As discussed above, properties in SFHAs with mortgages from federally regulated lenders must carry flood insurance. If, during the life of the loan, the property owner fails to purchase insurance, the lender must inform the owner that he or she must purchase flood insurance and

---

[8] As of January 2007, 85 WYO companies were actively issuing flood insurance policies (FEMA, undated). Policies can also be purchased directly from the NFIP through insurance agents.

[9] WYO companies report data on the policies in effect and claims paid monthly to the NFIP.

[10] NFIP policies are not available in communities that do not participate in the NFIP (although fewer than 5 percent of homes in the United States are outside NFIP communities) or within the coastal barrier resource system, including otherwise protected areas (see Tobin and Calfee, 2005, p. 48; and Dixon, Clancy, et al., 2006, p. 15).

[11] See Chubb (2006) for a description of Chubb's policy.

then purchase it on his or her behalf if the owner fails to do so.[12] Such lender-placed policies can be purchased from the NFIP, WYO companies, or private insurers.

In 1991, the NFIP introduced a special program to enable lenders to more easily force-place policies: the Mortgage Portfolio Protection Program (MPPP).[13] Less information on the property is required to issue an MPPP policy than for a standard flood insurance policy, but, for reasons that will be detailed later in this report, the MPPP policy is little used. As of July 2006, only 3,231 MPPP policies were in place (Scoville, 2006).[14] Instead, lenders, by and large, force-place policies underwritten by private sector insurers.

Actors in Lender-Placed Market

There are four primary actors in the lender-placed flood insurance market, and, as illustrated in Figure 1.1, their roles can overlap.

Lenders. Lenders create the demand for force-placed flood insurance policies. They are responsible for complying with the MPR[15] and also require borrowers to purchase flood and other types of hazard insurance (for example, fire or wind insurance) to reduce the risk of loan default due to adverse events.

Flood Determination Companies. Large and medium-sized, federally regulated lenders typically hire flood determination companies to identify whether each home in their loan

**Figure 1.1
Actors in the Lender-Placed Flood Insurance
Market**

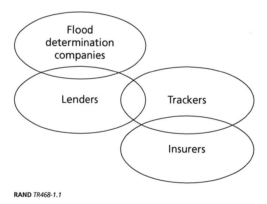

RAND *TR468-1.1*

---

[12] Lenders may fall out of compliance with the MPR because borrowers fail to renew their flood insurance policies during the course of a loan. Lenders may also fall out of compliance due to changes in the areas mapped as SFHAs. A home may be outside an SFHA when a loan is first issued and thus not subject to the MPR but then become subject to the MPR due to a map revision.

[13] The MPPP is available only through WYO companies that have agreed to participate in the NFIP's MPPP. Twenty-nine of the 85 insurers that participate in the WYO program offer the MPPP (FEMA, undated), and it is not available directly from the NFIP.

[14] Lenders rarely use a standard flood insurance policy to force-place insurance.

[15] Five federal regulators monitor compliance with the MPR (see Tobin and Calfee, p. 65).

portfolios lies inside an SFHA and thus must have flood insurance. Flood determination companies determine whether a property is in an SFHA based on FEMA's flood hazard maps, known as FIRMs. They also identify changes in flood zones that occur due to updating of flood maps subsequent to the initial flood zone determination (life of loan coverage). Some large lenders perform flood determinations in house (thus the overlap of the ovals in Figure 1.1), although those that do often rely on databases provided by flood determination companies. Flood determination companies generate revenue by charging a fee for each flood determination.

Trackers. Larger lenders also typically hire trackers to monitor whether the loans in their portfolios are carrying the appropriate types of insurance. Discussions with lenders and trackers suggest that smaller lenders frequently track insurance status in house, although quantitative data are not available on how often. Trackers usually monitor the status of all insurance required by the lenders, not just flood insurance. Trackers often charge a fee per loan tracked, although, if a tracker is part of a firm that also provides the insurance for properties found to have inadequate insurance, it will typically not charge a separate fee for tracking.

Insurers. Insurers issue flood insurance policies on properties that do not have the required flood insurance. They issue these policies at the lender's direction; the policies do not require homeowner consent. Insurers also commonly track loans (thus the overlap of the ovals in Figure 1.1), although some firms track loans but do not write insurance policies. Insurers investigate, process, and pay claims on the flood insurance policies. Some insurers hire outside firms to adjust claims, but the underwriting risk remains with the insurer. Insurers generate revenue through the premiums charged for their policies.

Previous Analysis of the Market Penetration Rate and the Number of Lender-Placed Policies

A previous RAND study estimated the proportion of single-family homes with flood insurance (the market penetration rate) and compliance with the MPR (Dixon, Clancy, et al., 2006). The study was based on detailed data on more than 27,000 single-family homes spread across 100 NFIP communities. The study concluded that 49 percent of single-family homes in SFHAs nationwide are protected by flood insurance.

Systematic, quantitative data on the number of lender-placed flood insurance policies are not available. Based on interviews with participants in the industry, FEMA estimated that 100,000 to 200,000 SFHA properties were insured through the private, non-NFIP lender–placed policies in 2004 (Thomas, 2004, p. 5). However, lack of information on the number of firms interviewed or on the type of data provided makes evaluating the reliability of this estimate difficult. Presumably, this estimate is for primary insurance policies and not private policies that add to the coverage of an existing NFIP policy (so-called *gap* or *coverage deficiency policies*). When Dixon, Clancy, et al. added this estimate of the number of private flood insurance policies to those that the NFIP underwrites, the market penetration rate for flood insurance for single-family homes in SFHAs rose from 49 percent to between 50 and 52 percent (Dixon, Clancy, et al., 2006, p. xiii).

While not as high as many would like, compliance with the MPR is considerable (Dixon, Clancy, et al., 2006). Dixon, Clancy, et al. found that 75 to 80 percent of homes subject to MPR nationwide are in compliance. As with the market penetration rate, the compliance rate varied considerably by region and appears higher in the South and West than in other parts of the country.

An MPR compliance rate substantially higher than the overall market penetration rate for flood insurance implies that the percentage of homeowners that buys flood insurance when not required to by the MPR is low. Dixon, Clancy, et al. (2006) estimate that approximately 45 percent of homes in SFHAs are not subject to the MPR and that only about 20 percent have flood insurance. This finding underscores the MPR's importance in determining the percentage of homes insured against flood.

Organization of This Report

The next chapter presents the methods used in our analysis. It describes the procedures used to identify and collect data from insurers, lenders, and trackers and provides an overview of the approaches used to extrapolate the findings on the number of private policies from the sample to the industry as a whole. The following three chapters report our findings. Chapter Three presents findings on the number of private policies force-placed on residential properties. Chapter Four describes the typical process for force-placing flood insurance policies and compares the policies offered by private insurers with those offered by the NFIP. It also evaluates the extent to which the private policies that lenders place meet MPR coverage requirements. Chapter Five examines what lenders, trackers, and insurers perceive to be the advantages of private insurance policies over NFIP policies. The final chapter of the report summarizes key findings and discusses their policy implications.

CHAPTER TWO

Study Methods

The analysis in this report is based on information collected from lenders, insurers, and trackers involved in the lender-placed market for residential flood insurance. We collected three different types of information from these groups. First, we assembled quantitative information on the number of lender-placed policies issued, the number of loans tracked, and related variables to project the size of the lender-placed market. Second, through in-person and telephone interviews, we elicited perceptions of the advantages and disadvantages of force-placing policies through the private market rather than through the NFIP. Finally, we collected samples of the insurance policies written by the private sector so that we could compare the terms and conditions of private policies with those of NFIP policies.

In this chapter, we first describe how we selected insurers, lenders, and trackers for the study and their participation rates. We then describe the methods used to collect the data. Finally, we turn to the approaches employed to project the number of lender-placed policies based on the study sample.

Sample Selection and Response Rates

We used separate procedures to recruit the samples of insurers, lenders, and trackers.

Insurer Sample

Based on conversations with knowledgeable parties in the lender-placed flood insurance market, we assembled an initial list of the insurers that write the largest number of lender-placed flood insurance policies. Our conversations suggested that eight insurers write the vast majority of lender-placed flood insurance policies.

We asked each of the eight insurers to participate in the study and to provide data on the number of lender-placed flood insurance policies currently in place, to complete an in-person or telephone interview, and to provide a copy of their lender-placed policy.

Six of the eight insurers agreed to interviews, and four of the eight provided quantitative data on the number of policies. We obtained insurance policies, either from the insurers themselves or from lenders, for five of the insurers. The policies obtained were current as of mid-2005. Factors that discouraged firms from participating include a scarcity of staff time and computing resources and concern about how the study results would be used. Some insurers feared that the NFIP's ultimate goal was to bring private policies back into the NFIP and did not want to be part of a study that, in their view, could threaten their business. We offered a written confidentiality agreement to each of the firms asked to participate in the study, but, even so, some insurers were also concerned about providing confidential information to a third party.

Lender Sample

We used a list from the Mortgage Bankers Association of the top 300 single-family home (one to four units) mortgage lenders ranked by number of 2003 home purchase originations to select a sample of lenders for the study. According to the Mortgage Bankers Association, these 300 lenders account for nearly 80 percent of annual loan originations nationwide (Mortgage Bankers, 2005). We divided lenders into three tiers based on size and selected a total of 18 lenders from the three tiers (see Table 2.1). We selected higher proportions of the lenders from the larger tiers to take advantage of the larger number of loans that these lenders issue.[1]

In each tier, the lenders selected were chosen from those lenders for which we had a point of contact. In some cases, project staff had a personal contact at the lending institution; in other cases, project staff had a contact who could then put us in touch with someone at the lender. The contacts for some lenders were compiled from attendance lists for flood insurance conferences.

As shown in Table 2.1, five of the 18 firms contacted (28 percent) agreed to provide quantitative data for the number of loans tracked and flood insurance policies placed. We completed interviews with three of the five, and another two lenders agreed to be interviewed but could not provide detailed enough quantitative data to be used in the study. The lenders contacted were not particularly concerned about how the NFIP might use the study results. They were concerned, however, about the staff and computing resources needed to assemble the data and sometimes concerned about providing confidential information to a third party.

Table 2.1
Sample of Lenders Selected for the Study

Number of Originations	Lenders in Top 300	Lenders Selected	Lenders Providing Quantitative Data
≥100,000	8	5	2
10,000 to 99,999	72	8	2
<10,000	200	5	1
Total	300	18	5

---

[1] The top eight lenders account for 32 percent of all originations, the next 72 lenders (lenders with between 10,000 and 99,999 originations) account for another 32 percent, and the remaining 200 for 36 percent (Mortgage Bankers Association, 2005).

Tracker Sample

Based on conversations with knowledgeable parties in the industry, we identified firms that track mortgages for flood insurance and other types of insurance. We identified seven trackers, and, during the course of the project, several of those interviewed expressed the belief that the top four account for a large percentage of total loans tracked by the tracking industry.[2]

We asked all seven of the trackers identified to participate in the study. Three of the top four and one of the remaining three agreed to provide quantitative data. We interviewed all of the top four trackers as well as the smaller tracker that provided quantitative data. Because most trackers also write flood insurance policies, there is substantial overlap among the trackers and the insurers participating in the study. In their capacity as trackers, trackers were not concerned about the NFIP's motives for the study, because they will continue to track loans regardless of whether policies are ultimately placed with the NFIP or in the private market. However, in their capacity as insurers, some firms were concerned about the study's possible ramifications on the future of their businesses.

Survey Procedures

Short survey instruments were developed to collect the quantitative data on the number of policies. Different forms were prepared for lenders, insurers, and trackers. A written confidentiality agreement was signed with all firms providing quantitative data. Data were requested on the number of lender-placed flood insurance policies currently in place and on the breakdown of the number of policies into primary and gap policies and by type of residential structure (single-family homes excluding condominium units, condominium units, and other residential structures).[3] Participating firms were also asked to report the data by state, if not too burdensome, and to indicate how often they force-place policies outside SFHAs and how often they write voluntary non-NFIP flood policies (never, infrequently, often, don't know). Finally, respondents were asked whether they could determine whether a policy was written on a first mortgage, second mortgage, or home equity line of credit, and project staff followed up on the response in subsequent phone calls.

We conducted most interviews in person and a few by phone. The interviews typically lasted one to two hours; at least two project members conducted all interviews on a confidential basis, following a semistructured interview protocol that allowed open-ended responses.

---

[2] As noted in Chapter One, some banks and other financial institutions do their own tracking, and we do not consider the number of self-tracked mortgages in estimating this market share.

[3] *Primary policies* are written when no other flood insurance policy is already in place on the property. *Gap policies* augment the coverage of primary policies. They may pay for losses between the policy limit of the primary policy and the loan amount or cover some of the deductible in the primary policy.

Methods for Estimating the Number of Lender-Placed Policies

Independent estimates of the number of lender-placed policies nationwide were constructed from the data provided by insurers, trackers, and lenders. We developed separate estimates of the number of primary and gap flood insurance policies written by private insurers. It is important to distinguish primary and gap policies when calculating how policies written by the private sector increase estimates of the market penetration rate of flood insurance. Including gap policies would bias estimates of market penetration upward because homes with gap policies would be double counted.

Below, we describe the approach for making projections from each data source. As will be discussed, each has strengths and weaknesses, and consistency of the various estimates increases confidence in the findings.

Projections Based on Insurer Data

Results on the number of policies written by the four insurers providing quantitative data were combined with the ranking of insurers by size developed by project staff to construct plausible ranges for the number of lender-placed policies written by the industry as a whole. The number of policies reported by the four firms was consistent with the initial ranking of firms by size, and the number of policies reported by the smallest insurer was not large.

To construct the upper bound of the plausible range, the largest number of policies that each of the four nonparticipating insurers could write and still preserve the firm-size ranking was determined.[4] The lower bound was calculated analogously, subject to the requirement that each firm wrote at least 500 policies. The high and low estimates for each of the eight firms were summed to create and plausible range for the industry as a whole.

This approach assumes that no other insurers in the industry write policies. However, given the low number of policies written by the smallest firm that did provide quantitative data for the study (and assuming that we have correctly identified the largest insurers in the lender-placed industry), it seems unlikely that including any additional insurers that might exist would significantly increase the estimated number of policies. Thus, the estimate of the number of policies based on insurer data will likely closely approximate the actual number of policies.

None of the insurers that provided data for the study could separate policies on second mortgages and home equity loans from policies on first mortgages. Thus, projections of the number of lender-placed policies based on insurer data include policies on all types of mortgages and home equity loans. The insurer data reflect policy counts as of dates between late 2004 and mid-2005, depending on insurer.

Projections Based on Lender Data

Although the number of lenders participating in the study is small relative to the total number of lenders in the country, the number of loans represented in the data provided is substantial. The five lenders participating in the study serviced about 8.7 million residential loans nation-

---

[4]   We could calculate the upper bound because we had data from the top-ranked insurer.

wide (regardless of flood zone), including condominiums. According to the American Housing Survey, there were 95 million housing units in the United States in structures with four or fewer units in 2005, including manufactured homes (U.S. Census Bureau, 2006, Table 1A-1).[5] Two-thirds of owner-occupied units, excluding manufactured homes, carry mortgages or home equity loans, and 43 percent of manufactured homes carry mortgages (U.S. Census Bureau, 2006, Table 3-15). If we assume that these mortgage rates apply to owner-occupied as well as to non–owner-occupied units,[6] then approximately 61 million homes in the United States have mortgages.[7] The 8.7 million loans represented in the sample thus amounts to approximately 14 percent of homes with residential mortgages nationwide.

To project the total number of lender-placed policies nationwide, the average placement rate (flood insurance policies written divided by the total number of loans) was multiplied by an estimate of the total number of primary mortgages serviced by lenders that are subject to the MPR (developed in Chapter Three). As shown in Table 2.1, larger lenders are overrepresented in the sample, and the placement rates calculated from the lender data were weighted to account for this oversampling.[8]

The data ultimately provided by the lenders that participated in the study varied a great deal in level of detail. Some lenders could provide information by state; others could not. Although one lender could report the number of second mortgages and home equity loans serviced and the number of flood insurance policies force-placed on them, the remaining lenders could not, because data on second mortgages and home equity loans were kept in separate parts of the organization from data on first mortgages and were difficult to access. Thus, in contrast to insurer estimates, the estimates of lender-placed policies based on lender data do not include policies written on second mortgages and home equity loans. Estimates of the number of policies on second mortgages and home equity loans appear in Chapter Three so that the reader can compare projections based on lender data with those based on insurer and

---

[5] The U.S. Census Bureau and the U.S. Department of Housing and Urban Development jointly conduct the American Housing Survey.

[6] About 60 percent of total housing units are owner occupied (U.S. Census Bureau, 2006, Table 1A-1).

[7] We ignore the difference between housing units in structures with two to four units and the number of structures. The number of structures is less than the number of units, and basing the number of mortgages on units would bias our estimate of the number of mortgages upward. However, to be comparable to the lender-provided data, the number of noncommercial housing units should include condominiums. Because condominiums can exist in buildings with more than four units, restricting attention to structures with four or fewer units introduces a downward bias in the estimate of the number of mortgages on residential structures, including condominiums. How the two biases offset is unknown. The two biases, however, are not particularly large. Even if every structure with two to four units had four units, the number of units in structures with one to four units (which we use here) would only be 9 percent greater than the number of structures with one to four units (94.8 million versus 87.3 million). Varying assumptions on the distribution of the 6.6 million condominiums reported in the American Housing Survey across structures categorized by number of units could, at most, decrease the number of housing units in structures with one to four units plus condominiums from 101.1 million to 94.8 million (9 percent).

[8] The average placement rate for the participating lenders in each of the three lender tiers identified above was weighted by the fraction of overall originations in that tier. The weights were 0.32 for the average placement rate of the two lenders with 100,000 or more originations, 0.32 percent for the average placement rate of the two lenders with 10,000 to 99,000, and 0.36 for the lender with fewer than 10,000 originations.

tracker data. The lender-provided data reflect policy counts as of dates between mid-2005 and early 2006, depending on the lender.

Even though the 8.7 million loans represented in the sample is a substantial number of loans, concern remains that the estimates of the number of lender-placed policies based on the lender data are subject to considerable uncertainty. A major concern is that only one lender in the sample is small (fewer than 10,000 originations). Small lenders account for roughly 36 percent of loans originated by the top 300 lenders and for the sizable number of loans issued by lenders that are not in the top 300 (lenders ranked 301 and below account for approximately 20 percent of total loans). Small lenders may have lower placement rates than larger lenders in part because, as suggested in Chapter One, smaller lenders are less likely to hire trackers. In addition to there being only one small lender in our sample, concern about bias in the estimate arises because the participating small lender is still among the largest 150 lenders nationwide and does use a tracker. The placement rate for the small lender in the sample may thus not be representative of all small lenders. Estimates of the number of lender-placed policies based on lender data must therefore be interpreted cautiously, although consistency of the estimates with estimates based on insurer and tracker data serve to increase confidence in conclusions about the number of lender-placed policies.

Projections Based on Tracker Data

The four trackers participating in the study tracked approximately 26 million loans on residential structures nationwide, including condominiums. As discussed, there do not appear to be a large number of tracking firms (seven were identified), so the trackers participating in the study represent a sizable portion of all loans tracked. One of the participating trackers estimated that tracking firms tracked a total of 50 million residential loans. Given this estimate, the firms participating in the study account for about one-half of the market.[9]

To extrapolate the findings for the sample to the industry as a whole, the average placement rate for the trackers in the study (weighted by the number of loans tracked by each tracker) was first calculated. The result was then applied to an estimate of the total number of loans with lenders subject to the MPR, including second mortgages and home equity loans. The total was again based on statistics from the American Housing Survey.

Trackers could not distinguish first mortgages from second mortgages and home equity loans, and thus the data on loans tracked and policies placed reflect all types of mortgages and home equity loans. The tracker-provided data were as of dates between late 2004 and mid-2005.

Like estimates based on data from lenders, it is reasonable to expect that, if anything, estimates of the number of lender-placed policies based on tracker data will overstate the actual number of lender-placed policies. Our extrapolation approach assumes that the placement rate for tracked loans is the same as for untracked loans. However, banks that do their own tracking may not have as thorough of a tracking system as firms that specialize in tracking. In the

---

[9]   These numbers also imply that the majority of homes with mortgages are tracked. The 50 million tracked mortgages amount to 82 percent of the 61 million homes with mortgages.

next chapter, we examine whether any empirical evidence supports the hypothesis that placement rates are lower for lenders that track loans in house.

Characterizing Uncertainty

We constructed ranges into which the number of lender-placed policies could plausibly fall based on reasonable assumptions about the underlying parameters. We did not assign a probability that the actual number of policies would fall into such intervals. Rather, these intervals are meant to convey a sense of the rough magnitude of the actual number of policies. Consistency of estimates derived from the different data sources increase the confidence in the estimates.

Given the small sample sizes, we determined that quantitative statistical analysis of the findings (i.e., calculation of confidence intervals) would not add a great deal of value to the study. Even though the sample sizes are small, however, it does not follow that the reader should have little confidence in the findings. The number of insurers participating in the study is small, but a substantial part of the industry is represented. The situation for trackers is similar. In addition, we compare the estimates across the different data sources, and consistency of the findings increase confidence in the accuracy of the results.

CHAPTER THREE

Size of the Lender-Placed Market for Residential Properties

In this chapter, we present findings on the number of placed policies, comparing results based on data from insurers, lenders, and trackers. The estimates are for policies on residential properties. They do not include policies that private insurers write on commercial and industrial properties or on structures with more than four housing units.

Market Size Based on Insurer Data

The four insurers participating in the study reported a total of approximately 100,000 primary lender–placed flood insurance policies in effect on residential structures at the time of the survey. The total covers residential structures with one to four units and includes condominiums and mobile homes. The number of condominiums and mobile homes is low, however, with respondents reporting that policies on these two types of units accounted for less than 5 percent of the total.

The reported number of primary policies includes policies written on second mortgages and home equity loans in addition to policies written on first mortgages. Policies in California, Florida, Louisiana, and Texas were most heavily represented in the sample.

Some of the insurers participating in the survey wrote gap policies in addition to primary policies. We have excluded estimates of the number of gap policies from the 100,000 total. One insurer reported that gap policies amount to roughly 20 percent of the primary lender–placed policies. Several others acknowledged that they wrote gap policies but could not provide information on the number of such policies.

The four insurers participating in the study were among the largest private underwriters of flood insurance in the market. When we extrapolate the findings to the market as a whole using the methods discussed in Chapter Two, we estimate that between 128,000 and 187,000 primary flood insurance policies are written on residential structures nationwide.

We were not able to obtain extensive data on growth in the number of lender-placed policies over time. One insurer participating in the study, however, noted that the number of lender-placed policies grew between 1994 and 2001 but had remained flat since 2001. The 1994 legislation that strengthened the MPR likely drove growth in policies. Growth in the number of private policies likely leveled off as compliance with the MPR gradually increased.

Market Size Based on Lender Data

Approximately 26,000 primary lender–placed flood insurance policies were in effect on the 8.7 million loans serviced by the five lenders participating in the study, which amounts to 0.30 percent of loans serviced.[1] Lender-placed flood insurance policies as a percent of loans tracked did not vary a great deal among the five lenders in the study. These figures do not include second mortgages and home equity loans or the policies force-placed on them.[2]

Overall, about 4 percent of the loans serviced were in SHFAs.[3] Nearly all lender-placed flood insurance policies were placed on loans in SFHAs, with the result that private flood insurance policies were placed on 7.5 percent of loans serviced in SFHAs.

The data provided by lenders suggest that there are a sizable number of gap policies in addition to primary insurance policies. Two of the five lenders reported almost equal numbers of gap and primary policies. One lender reported a smaller number of gap policies relative to primary policies, and the final two lenders did not report any gap policies. It is unknown, however, whether the latter two lenders did not force-place gap policies or placed gap policies but could not report the number. Overall, gap policies amounted to about 40 percent of the total number of primary flood insurance policies that the five lenders reported.

As reported in Chapter Two, roughly 61 million homes in the United States have mortgages, and previous work has suggested that 80 to 90 percent of mortgages are with lenders subject to the MPR (Dixon, Clancy, et al. 2006, p. 22). Assuming that 85 percent of loans are with lenders subject to the MPR leads to the conclusion that approximately 52 million of the 61 million mortgages are with lenders that are subject to the MPR.

When weighted to account for the variation in the placement rate by lender size (see Chapter Two), the placement rate declines from 0.30 percent to 0.21 percent. Applying this placement rate to the 52 million mortgages serviced by lenders subject to the MPR implies that there are approximately 110,000 private lender–placed flood insurance policies (0.21 percent of 52 million mortgages).[4]

Based on the limited data provided by the lenders participating in the study on gap policies, the number of gap policies could plausibly equal 40 percent of the number of primary policies, or an additional 44,000 policies. The number could conceivably be higher if the lenders reporting no gap policies did force-place gap policies but could not provide data on them.

---

[1]   The 8.7 million figure includes loans that are inside as well as loans that are outside SFHAs.

[2]   We did not receive detailed data on the number of second mortgages and home equity loans tracked or the number of policies placed on them, but the survey responses suggested that the number of such loans was not negligible. One tracker reported that second mortgages and home equity loans accounted for 20 percent of loans tracked, and an insurer reported often placing policies on second mortgages and home equity loans. We further address the issue of second mortgages and home equity loans later in the chapter.

[3]   This percentage is somewhat lower than previous findings on the proportion of homes in SFHAs. Dixon, Clancy, et al. found that 4.5 percent of single-family homes were in SHFAs (2006, p. 16) and Tobin and Calfee (2005, p. 118) found that 5.5 percent of flood-zone determinations made by large national flood determination companies were in SFHAs. Tobin and Calfee's estimate may be biased upward for reasons discussed in Dixon, Clancy, et al. (2006, p. 16).

[4]   By applying the 0.21-percent placement rate only to an estimate of loans not subject to the MPR, we assume, in effect, that banks that service loans not subject to the MPR do not check the loans in their portfolios for flood insurance.

Market Size Based on Tracker Data

About 55,000 primary lender–placed flood insurance policies were in effect on the 26 million loans tracked by the four trackers participating in the study, representing 0.21 percent of loans serviced. Flood insurance policies as a percent of loans tracked did not vary a great deal across the four trackers in the study.

The 0.21-percent placement rate for trackers is identical to the weighted placement rate that lenders reported on the loans they service. It is not too surprising that the placement rates are similar, because, for the most part, the lenders participating in the study hired the same trackers that participated in the study. However, the two placement rates are not directly comparable, because the data from the trackers include second mortgages and home equity loans, while the data from the lenders do not.

To extrapolate the findings to the nation as a whole, we multiply the tracker placement rate by an estimate of the total number of mortgages, both primary and secondary, and home equity loans. The findings of the American Housing Survey suggest that the combined number of primary, secondary, and home equity loans is approximately 33 percent greater than the number of primary mortgages alone.[5] Increasing the 52 million estimate above of the number of primary loans at lenders subject to the MPR by that 33 percent results in approximately 69 million mortgages. Applying the tracker placement rate then implies that there are approximately 142,000 primary lender–placed policies on residential housing units.

Several of the trackers interviewed indicated that gap policies were also written on the loans they tracked, but only one of the four firms could provide information on the number of gap policies. The tracker data are thus insufficient to construct an estimate of gap policies.

Implications

Table 3.1 summarizes estimates of the number of primary lender–placed flood insurance policies underwritten by the private sector based on data from insurers, lenders, and trackers. The estimate based on lender data is lower than estimates from the other two sources likely in part because it does not include primary policies placed on second mortgages and home equity loans, while estimates based on the other two data sources do. If, as suggested above, the combined number of first and second mortgages and home equity loans is 33 percent greater than the number of primary mortgages, then adding in the number of policies placed by lenders on second mortgages and home equity loans could plausibly increase the lender-based estimate

---

[5] For owner-occupied housing units with mortgages and home equity loans, the American Housing Survey divides the units into those with one mortgage or home equity loan, those with two such loans, those with three or more such loans, and those for which the number of loans was not reported. We calculated the total number of mortgages and home equity loans by first assuming that each of the homes reporting three or more loans actually had three loans and then assuming that they had six loans (which seems like a plausible upper limit for the average number of loans for homes in this category). We also assumed that homes for which the number of loans was not reported (about 10 percent of the total) split among the other categories in proportion to the distribution of homes for which the number of loans was available. The result of these calculations is that the number of loans is 30 to 36 percent greater than the number of homes with at least one loan. We use the midpoint of this range in our projections of the number of lender-placed policies, based on loans tracked.

Table 3.1
Estimated Number of Primary Lender–Placed Flood Insurance Policies Written by Private Insurers

Source of Data Used for Estimate	Policies in Place (thousands)
Insurers	128–187
Lenders	
Excluding second mortgages and home equity loans	110
With adjustment to account for second mortgages and home equity loans	154
Trackers	142

NOTE: Estimates reflect policies in place some time between mid-2004 and early 2006.

from 110,000 to 154,000.[6] Such a correction, however, assumes that the placement rate on second mortgages and home equity loans by lenders is the same as for first mortgages.

Each of the estimates is subject to considerable uncertainty. Estimates based on insurer data are subject to uncertainty because we have only crude ways to estimate the market share accounted for by the insurers that participated in the study. For both lenders and trackers, we apply the policy placement rates for the firms participating in the survey to an estimate of the total number of mortgages. There is some reason to expect that, if anything, the resulting projections for lenders and trackers are too high. The lenders that provided data for the study all had very well-developed programs for monitoring their loans. Other lenders may not have such well-developed programs and their placement rates may be lower. Similarly, our interviews indicated that smaller banks often track loans themselves and the thoroughness of their tracking procedures may not be as high as firms that specialize in tracking. Given that the estimates based on the lender and tracker data fall in or very close to the range estimated from lender data, however, the findings do not provide strong evidence that the placement rates for lenders not participating in the study are substantially lower than those that did participate in the study or that results of in-house tracking differ markedly from those of external trackers.

Limitations on the American Housing Survey data also add uncertainty to the estimates based on lender and tracker data. As discussed, the estimate used here of the total number of residential structures (four units or fewer) plus condominiums might be too high or too low, and the ratio of second mortgages and home equity loans to first mortgages can only be approximated. These uncertainties, however, are not particularly significant.

In spite of the underlying uncertainties, the three estimates agree on the rough order of magnitude for the number of lender-placed policies on residential properties. Once we adjust the lender estimate to account for second mortgages and home equity loans, the number of policies based on the lender data is similar to the number of policies based on the tracker data and is well within the range developed from the insurer data. Consistency of the findings provides confidence that on the order of 130,000 to 190,000 primary lender–placed flood insurance policies are in effect at any one time.

---

[6] The 154,000 estimate results from multiplying 110,000 by 1.33.

Including gap policies increases the number of lender-placed flood insurance policies underwritten by the private sector, but the data provided on gap policies are spotty. Lender-provided data point to a substantial number of gap policies, perhaps equal to 40 percent of the number of primary policies. Insurers and trackers provided inadequate information to estimate the number of gap policies. If the number of gap policies did amount to 40 percent of primary policies, the number of primary and gap policies combined written by private insurers in the lender-placed market would be in the 180,000 to 260,000 range (1.4 times the range for primary policies based on insurer data). This prediction is quite speculative, however, and further investigation of the number of gap policies is warranted.

Our estimates do not capture all of the non-NFIP flood insurance policies written by the private market. They include policies written in the lender-placed market but not those written in the voluntary residential market. The private residential voluntary market is thought to be small, but further study on the size of this market is warranted. The estimates also do not include commercial policies. Commercial policies often include coverage for flood, and the number of such policies is likely sizable. One of the trackers interviewed reported that 20 percent of the loans it tracked were on commercial properties; however, our interview respondents commented that policies were seldom force-placed on commercial loans. Further work is needed on the size of both the voluntary and force-placed private market for commercial policies.

CHAPTER FOUR

Procedures for Force-Placing Flood Insurance Policies and the Features of Private Policies

Many lenders have put in place well-developed processes for monitoring whether the homes in their loan portfolios comply with the MPR and for force-placing flood insurance policies on those that do not. This chapter draws on interviews with lenders, trackers, and insurers to describe the typical procedures for force-placing policies on residential properties. The procedures are largely consistent among the lenders interviewed, although, as noted in Chapter One, the division of responsibilities among the different actors can vary. We note some of the more significant ways in which procedures can depart from the typical process described below.

To satisfy the MPR, lenders must use insurance policies at least as comprehensive as those that the NFIP offers and purchase specified amounts of insurance. In this chapter, we also summarize findings from the interviews on the amount of coverage placed. Finally, we draw on both the interviews and our analysis of five private policies to compare terms and conditions of private policies with those of the policy available through the MPPP. In addition to allowing an assessment of whether policies meet the conditions of the MPR, this comparison provides a backdrop for the analysis in Chapter Five of stakeholder perceptions of the advantages private policies have over the MPPP program when force-placing insurance.

Process for Issuing Lender-Placed Policies

Figure 4.1 depicts the typical process for issuing a lender-placed policy. Lenders hire flood determination companies to determine the flood zone for new loans and to notify them of flood zone changes for existing loans that result from NFIP flood map changes.[1] Lenders then send data on their loan portfolio, with flood zone detail attached, to the trackers. It is not uncommon for lenders to transmit an updated file to trackers every two weeks. As discussed in Chapter One, some lenders, usually thought to be smaller ones, track the status of insurance on their loans in house.

Insurers writing policies on homes with mortgages (covering fire, flood, wind, and other perils) typically notify the lender when a policy is renewed. The lender's tracker often receives these notices directly via post office boxes that the lender sets up. Based on these renewal notifications, the tracker then determines whether the required insurance is in force. If the

---

[1] Flood determination companies can provide a one-time flood determination for a property or provide an initial flood determination and then monitor the property for flood zone changes over the life of the loan.

Figure 4.1
Typical Process for Force-Placing Flood Insurance on Residential Properties

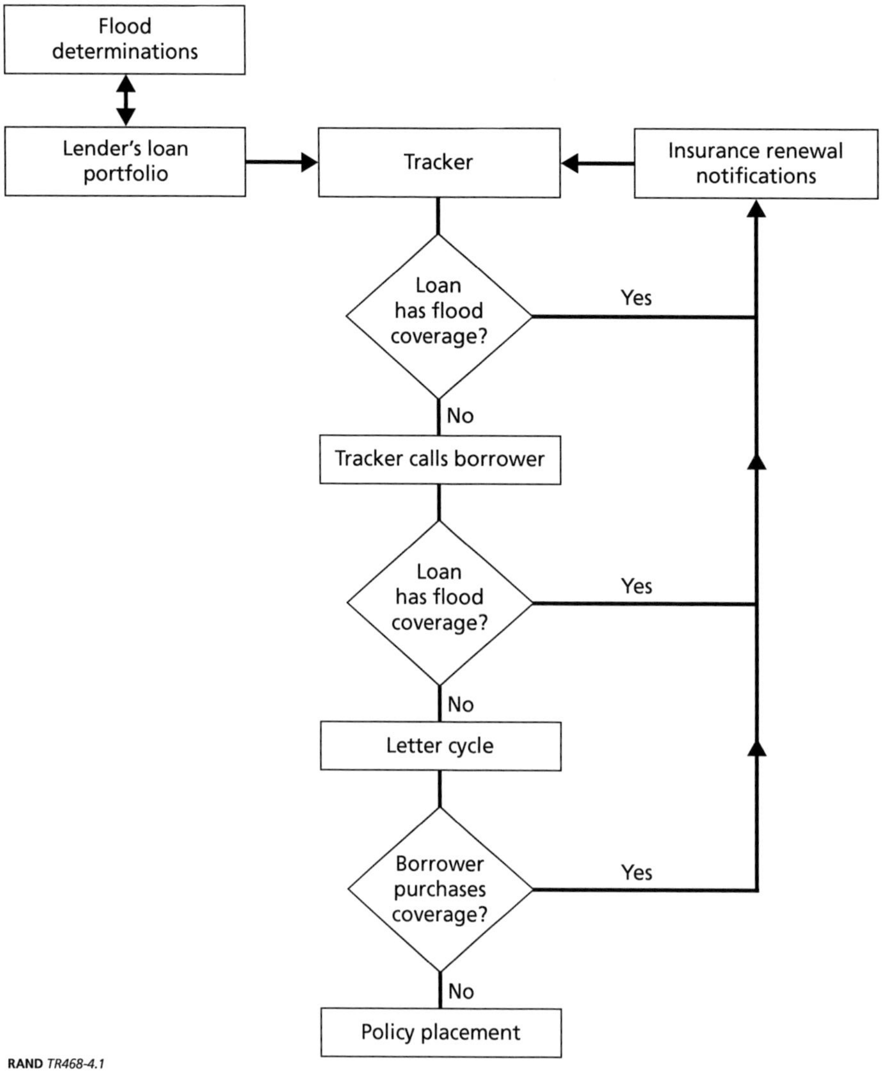

RAND *TR468-4.1*

tracker does not receive a renewal notification for flood insurance, it begins the process of force-placing a policy.[2] In some cases, the lender processes the insurance renewals and then transmits the information on insurance noncompliance to the trackers.

Several of the trackers we interviewed first telephone the borrower to confirm that the flood insurance policy has not been renewed. This practice has been found to substantially reduce the number of unnecessary force placements. If the tracker cannot confirm that the borrower has renewed coverage, it begins the letter cycle. The letter cycle typically consists of three letters. The tracker sends the first at least 45 days before policy placement and the second

---

[2] Because the MPR must be satisfied before a loan can be issued, there are almost no lender-placed policies at loan origination.

15 to 30 days after the first. The letters inform the borrower of the flood insurance requirement, the lapse in coverage, and options for purchasing policies from the NFIP and then go on to inform the borrower that the lender will buy flood insurance on the borrower's behalf if he or she does not purchase flood insurance. The final letter accompanies a flood insurance certificate and informs the borrower that the lender has force-placed an insurance policy.

Not all lenders require trackers to call borrowers before initiating the letter cycle. Also, in some cases, the insurer conducts the call and implements the letter cycle instead of the tracker (this commonly happens when a lender tracks its own loans and works directly with an insurer).

Federal regulations require 45 days to pass between initial notification and force placement (FEMA, 1999, p. 38). Thus trackers typically place a policy on the 46th day after initial notification. If an escrow account exists for the loan (and several lenders interviewed said that the majority of their loans have escrow accounts), then the lender adds the policy premium to the escrow account. Otherwise, the lender increases the monthly loan payment to cover the cost of the insurance. The lenders and trackers we interviewed reported that the process for force-placing policies is the same for first mortgages, second mortgages, and home equity loans. Based on interview responses, trackers commonly force-place policies on about one-third of the properties for which they start the letter cycle.

Few lender-placed policies remain in force for the entire one-year term. As will be discussed, force-placed policies are substantially more expensive than standard NFIP policies, inducing most policyholders to replace their lender-placed policy with a standard NFIP policy. Based on the interviews, it is not uncommon for half the policies to be cancelled within 90 days and two-thirds cancelled by the end of the one-year policy term (the stick rate). In one respondent's experiences, only 10 percent of lender-placed policies are renewed. However, the experiences on stick rate and renewal rates are not consistent across insurers. One large insurer believed that more than 50 percent of the force-placed policies are renewed.

There does not appear be a standard process for renewing lender-placed policies.[3] According to one large tracker, some lenders require a letter cycle before a policy can be renewed, while others do not. Another stakeholder said that NFIP regulations were not clear on whether a letter cycle was required and that his firm chose not to require one. When a lender requires one for renewals, the letter cycle can be timed so that the policy is renewed on the expiration date. One lender started the letter cycle 60 days before the lender-placed policy was set to expire and then renewed the policy on the expiration date if the borrower did not provide evidence of flood insurance.

Lender Coverage Requirements

Consistent with MPR provisions, lenders usually require flood insurance on the home structure equal to the least of (1) $250,000 (the NFIP maximum for structure coverage), (2) the

---

[3]   Although the MPPP policy is an annual policy and cannot be renewed, it can be rewritten each year if the required procedures (i.e., the full letter cycle) are followed.

unpaid mortgage balance, and (3) the replacement value of the home. Surprisingly, according to some trackers, the loan portfolio database provided to trackers often does not include information on replacement cost. In such cases, insurers typically force-place coverage equal to the lesser of $250,000 and the outstanding loan balance.

Some lenders require flood insurance with the same coverage limits as fire insurance, up to $250,000. Insurers usually write fire insurance policies for the replacement value of the home.[4] This standard is referred to as *equal hazard insurance* and is a more stringent standard than the MPR requires.[5]

None of the lenders we interviewed force-placed flood insurance policies outside SFHAs (at least intentionally). Lenders can, in principle, require flood insurance on homes outside SFHAs as part of the condition for a loan, but it appears that few do so.

Some insurers offer only structure coverage, while others offer both structure and contents coverage. Insurers reported, however, that contents coverage is only very rarely force-placed.

Comparison of Private Policies and Policies Available Through the Mortgage Portfolio Protection Plan

To satisfy the MPR, a private policy "should guarantee that the flood insurance coverage, considering both deductibles and exclusions or conditions offered by the insurer, is at least as broad as the coverage offered by the NFIP policy" (FEMA, 1999, p. 11-1).[6] Table 4.1 compares the policies available in the private market with those that the NFIP offers. Features that pertain to placement, termination, and other administrative issues are presented first, followed by features that pertain to the types of risks covered. The final set of features describes the types of losses that private and the standard NFIP policies cover. The second column of Table 4.1 describes the policy available through the MPPP, and the third column summarizes the features of the five policies reviewed for this study.[7] The last column compares the private policy

---

[4] Fannie Mae and Freddie Mac require fire insurance for the replacement value of the home.

[5] Lenders might require a more stringent flood insurance standard to provide greater protection for the assets securing the loan. Borrowers, not the lender, must pay for the insurance, and thus the cost to lenders of requiring higher policy limits is small. (In principle, requiring more coverage could be costly to a lender if it induced borrowers to switch to a lender that does not require additional coverage or if higher insurance payments increased the probability that the borrower would default on the mortgage.)

[6] The NFIP has issued guidance, as opposed to regulations, for using private policies to meet the MPR. The guidance states that private policies on residential properties should (a) be written by insurers licensed to do business in the jurisdiction in which the property is located; (b) be as restrictive in their cancellation provisions as the NFIP, which restricts cancellation of a policy to only a very few limited conditions; (c) contain a mortgage interest clause similar to that contained in the NFIP policy, which provides that coverage shall continue in force for the benefit of the mortgagee (lender) for 30 days after written notice of cancellation; and (d) contain a provision providing the insured with at least 12 months after mailing of notice of disallowance or partial disallowance of a claim within which to file any suit against the insurer (FEMA, 1999, p. 11-1). We did not systemically investigate the extent to which private policies satisfy these other four criteria. However, evidence of shortcomings in these dimensions did not arise during the course of our interviews.

[7] The policy available through the MPPP is the NFIP's standard flood insurance policy.

with the MPPP policy, indicating whether the private policies are broader or more flexible than the MPPP policy. The policies reviewed were all current as of mid-2005.

Administrative Features

Information Required to Issue Policy. Private insurers typically require only the borrower's name, mailing address, property address, flood zone, flood map panel number and suffix, occupancy type (residential or commercial), loan number, and loan amount to force-place a residential policy. Some insurers will issue a policy when the flood zone is missing. In such cases, the flood zone defaults to an A zone. The amount of information required to write an MPPP policy is comparable to that required by private policies; however, lenders must specify the flood zone (see first row of Table 4.1).[8]

Named Insured. The lender is the named insured on private policies, whereas the homeowner and the lender or lenders are the named insureds on the MPPP policy. Although the named insured differs between the two types of policies, one convention does not seem broader or more flexible than the other.

Policy Effective Date. Backdating is a standard feature of private flood insurance policies that helps lenders hedge risk to their loan portfolios. It also protects homeowners against losses that occur during the letter cycle. The NFIP allows a 30-day grace period on its policies, which means that flood coverage remains in effect as long as the policyholder renews the policy within 30 days of the policy expiration date.[9] The 45-day waiting period means that, even with the 30-day grace period, the lender's collateral is at risk of uninsured losses for 15 days. Backdating means that the private flood insurance policy takes effect at the initiation of the letter cycle, not when the policy is placed. As shown in the first row of Table 4.1, MPPP policies do not allow backdating.

Automatic Coverage Endorsement. Insurers typically write a master policy with the lender as the named insured and then issue a separate certificate in the name of the borrower when insurance is force-placed.[10] Private insurers usually offer what is referred to as an automatic coverage endorsement to lenders whose portfolios meet certain requirements.[11] The endorsement, also sometimes referred to as a compliance endorsement, is offered at little or no charge, and lenders, particularly the larger ones, usually purchase it. When automatic

---

[8] Applications for the standard NFIP policy require considerably more information than applications for private policies or MPPP policies. Standard NFIP policies can require an elevation certificate, pictures of the structure, information on the number of floors, whether there is a basement or enclosure below the lowest living floor, and whether the home is a pre-FIRM or a post-FIRM structure. An elevation certificate is typically required for post-FIRM structures and verifies the elevation data of a structure relative to the ground level. A professional surveyor must issue it. Elevation certificates typically cost on the order of $300 if done at the time of purchase and in conjunction with a home survey. If done alone, the cost can run much higher, depending on where the home is situated and the location of the nearest elevation marker.

[9] The NFIP requires a 30-day waiting period on new flood insurance policies, but this waiting period is waived for lender-placed loans (NFIP, ongoing, p. GR-8; FEMA, 1999, pp. 24, 38).

[10] Because the master policy is with a lender, insurers consider lender-placed flood insurance a commercial rather than a personal line of business.

[11] Typically, lenders must have an automated tracking system that tracks loans for evidence of insurance rather than just react to cancellation notices from insurers.

Table 4.1
Comparison of Five Private Flood Insurance Policies with the MPPP Policy

Policy Feature	NFIP's MPPP Policy	Five Private Policies	Comparison
1. Administrative features			
Information needed to issue policy	Owner name, property address, mailing address, flood map panel number and suffix, flood zone, occupancy, lender, amt. of coverage	Similar to MPPP except for some policies flood zone will default to A if unknown[a]	0/+
Named insured	Property owner and lender(s)	Lender	0
Effective date	Policy not effective until end of 45-day letter cycle	Able to backdate typically for 30 to 60 days	+
Automatic coverage endorsement	Not available	Usually available	+
Gap coverage	Not available	Available	+
Renewals	Not renewable, but can be rewritten if notification procedures followed	Continues to renew until cancellation or loan sold (borrower receives renewal notices from the lender, however)	+
Cancellation	Requires signature of homeowner to cancel	Does not require homeowner signature to cancel	+
Eligible areas	NFIP participating communities only, not available in Coastal Barrier Resource Act (CBRA) zones	Participating, nonparticipating, and suspended NFIP communities; some offer coverage in CBRA zones	+
Statute of limitations on claims	12 months after denial of claim	Some same as MPPP, others require suit to be brought within 12 months of date of loss	0/–
2. Risks covered			
Flood	Affects two or more acres or two or more properties affected	Similar definition	0
Mudflows	Covered	Covered	0
Mudslides	Not covered	Covered	+
Earth movement	No coverage for landslide, land subsidence, sinkholes	Similar exclusion	0
Mold damage	Excluded if due to policyholder failure to inspect and maintain property after flood waters recede	Some policies have similar exclusion; others have absolute mold or microorganism exclusion	0/–
Pollutants	No coverage for testing or monitoring but cleanup covered	No coverage for testing, monitoring, or cleanup	–

Table 4.1—Continued

Policy Feature	NFIP's MPPP Policy	Five Private Policies	Comparison
3. Losses covered			
Structure coverage limit	$250,000	Varies across policies, $1–$2 million common for residential	+
Type of home eligible for replacement cost	Primary, single-family homes only	Some allow on one- to four-family structures regardless of whether primary; others follow MPPP policy	0/+
Coverage requirement to be eligible for replacement cost	Insured to 80 percent of replacement cost or $250,000	Same as MPPP for some policies; others pay replacement cost of up to policy limit with no requirement on amount of insurance in force	0/+
Additional living expenses	Not covered	Some provide no coverage; others allow up to $1,000	0/+
Basement	Excludes finishing of drywall and painting and floors; includes sunken room or portion of room in definition of *basement*	Some do not include sunken room or portion of room in definition of *basement*; others use same language as NFIP	0/+
Detached structures	Covers only detached garages; coverage limited to 10 percent of policy limit; payments counted toward policy limit	Broader definition of *structures covered*; some allow additional 10% coverage for detached structures; others count payments against policy limit	+
Condominium association assessments	Will not pay if association is underinsured or for association deductible	Will pay for assessments due to deductible or underinsurance	+
Items considered part of structure	Items such as refrigerators, cooking ranges, ovens, and awnings covered	Comparable to MPPP	0
Deductible	$500	$750 common but varies across policies	–
Contents coverage limit	$100,000[b]	Not available because lender does not have insurable interest in contents[c]	–
Debris removal	Included within structure coverage limits	Same as MPPP for some policies; others have $1,000 limit	0/–
Loss avoidance measures	Up to $1,000 for costs for items such as sandbags and labor	Most policies same as MPPP; some with $500 limit	0/–
Increased cost of compliance coverage limit	$30,000	$15,000 to $30,000[d]	0/–

Table 4.1—Continued

NOTE: + = private policies are broader or more flexible than MPPP policy. – = private policies are less broad or less flexible than MPPP policy. 0 = private policies are comparable to MPPP policy. 0/+ = some private policies are comparable and some are broader or more flexible than MPPP policy. 0/– = some are comparable and some are less broad or less flexible than MPPP policy.

[a] SFHAs are composed of A zones and V zones. V zones are areas subject to wave velocity (usually from wind-blown ocean waves), whereas A zones are not.

[b] Contents coverage is rarely force-placed, and, under MPPP, lenders may be able to force-place only if contents in part secure the loan.

[c] While none of the five policies reviewed allowed for contents coverage, some of the stakeholders interviewed reported that some private carriers would write contents coverage if requested.

[d] Limits for some insurers in effect as of 2005 and may have been increased since then.

coverage is in place, a primary mortgage that is subject to the NFIP's MPR is covered as soon as information on the property is transferred from the lender to the tracker. If a property that should have flood insurance but does not experiences a flood loss, the property is automatically covered for losses up to the amount of the outstanding loan balance. The endorsement requires that the applicable premium for the property be netted out before payment is made to the lender. Automatic coverage, like backdating, protects lenders from periods when loans in their portfolios are uninsured from flood and protects homeowners from periods where their property is uninsured. The NFIP does not offer automatic coverage.[12]

Gap Coverage. As discussed in Chapter Two, gap policies augment the coverage provided by a primary flood insurance policy. Gap coverage is also referred to as *deficiency coverage*. Private insurers offer both primary and gap policies. The NFIP does not offer gap policies because a property can have only one NFIP policy.

Most of the stakeholders we interviewed said that lenders frequently do not force-place gap policies. When flood insurance did not meet the lender requirements, some lenders send out a "soft" notice letter that informs the borrower that coverage is inadequate, but they take no action if the borrower does not increase the amount of coverage.

Some lenders do regularly force-place gap policies. One of the lenders interviewed requires that the policy deductible not exceed the greater of 1 percent of the policy limit or $1,000. This condition often is not met, and this lender consequently force-places a considerable number of gap policies. An insurer and tracker indicated that the interest in gap policies was increasing and that his firm planned to begin force-placing gap policies by the end of 2005.

Renewals. The MPPP policy is a one-year policy that can be renewed only after a full 45-day notification process.[13] In contrast, private policies typically continue to renew until they are cancelled. Thus, as far as the private insurers are concerned, there is no need to provide a 45-day notice before a private policy can be renewed. As discussed, lenders have differing opinions about whether notification is required to renew a lender-placed policy, but, in any case,

---

[12] During the interviews, we also heard reports of some insurers now providing deficiency coverage as a type of automatic coverage endorsement (referred to in this case as *blanket coverage*, for which lenders, not borrowers, pay).

[13] NFIP documents are not clear on whether the renewal process must wait until the initial MPPP policy expires (NFIP, ongoing, p. MPPP-5). It may be possible to start the renewal process 45 days before the expiration of the MPPP policy.

the ability of private policies to remain in force until cancelled provides flexibility and ease of handling to lenders and trackers that the MPPP policy does not.

Cancellation. Given the substantial percentage of lender-placed policies that are cancelled not long after being issued (presumably because the borrower has obtained a cheaper NFIP policy), the requirements for cancelling a policy are important to both lenders and insurers. The NFIP requires a signature from the borrower before an MPPP policy can be cancelled (NFIP, ongoing, p. MPPP-6, CN-7). Private insurers require only notification from the lender, not the borrower's signature, because the master policy is written in the lender's name.

Eligible Areas. In contrast to the NFIP, all of the insurers interviewed are willing to write policies in participating, nonparticipating, and suspended NFIP communities. Some also offer coastal barrier resource system (CBRS) policies in areas within the CBRS, including otherwise protected areas (again in contrast to the NFIP).

Statute of Limitations on Claims. The NFIP allows policyholders one year to file a lawsuit or otherwise contest a claim denial or payment. The statute of limitations begins to toll on the date that the insurer denies the claim or makes a payment. Private policies also give the policyholder 12 months to contest a claim payment or denial, but the statute of limitations runs from the date of the loss (i.e., the date of the flood event). Recall that the policyholder on private policies is the lender, while, on MPPP policies, it is the homeowner and lender(s). Thus, the lender must bring the claim under private policies, while the homeowner or lender(s) could bring a claim under the MPPP policy.

Summary. As demonstrated by the last column in Table 4.1, the administrative and lender protection features of private policies are, for the most part, more flexible or broader than those of the MPPP policy. Private insurers offer several optional endorsements and provide features that enhance the lender's ability to tailor the coverage to its portfolio's particular characteristics. The only aspect in which private policies are more limited than MPPP policies is in provisions that govern the appeal of claims payments.

Risks Covered

Private policies provided broader coverage for some risks than the MPPP policy but provided less broad coverage for other risks. The second set of rows in Table 4.1 compares the hazards covered by the two sets of policies. For example, private policies cover mudslides, while the MPPP policy does not. On the other hand, some private policies have stronger mold exclusions than the MPPP policy does. In addition, none of the private policies reviewed covers testing, monitoring, or cleanup of pollution that occurs during a flood event, while the MPPP policy covers cleanup even though it excludes coverage for testing and monitoring.

Losses Covered

We now compare the types of and limits on losses that private and MPPP policies cover. As shown in the last column of the third section of Table 4.1, the private policies examined compare favorably with the MPPP policy in several dimensions but come up short in a few others.

Higher policy limits for structure coverage are available in the private market than from the NFIP. The NFIP offers a maximum $250,000 in structure coverage on residential buildings and individual condominium units, whereas some insurers are willing to provide $1 million or more in coverage.

Private and MPPP policies differ in terms of the circumstances in which they pay replacement cost (up to the policy limit) for damage due to flood as opposed to the depreciated value (or actual cash value) of the damaged components of the building structure. MPPP policies pay replacement cost only on single-family homes that serve as a primary residence. Some private policies follow suit, but others will pay replacement cost regardless of whether the structure has two, three, and four units and regardless of whether the home serves as a primary residence (a vacation home or rental home, for example).[14] MPPP policies also have requirements on the amount of coverage that must be in place before paying replacement cost. MPPP policies will pay replacement cost (up to the policy limit) if the structure is insured for at least 80 percent of the replacement cost (again up to $250,000).[15] Some private policies have similar requirements, but others will pay replacement cost regardless of the amount of coverage in place, subject to the policy limit.[16]

As seen in Table 4.1, private policies meet or exceed the features of the MPPP policy in several other dimensions. The MPPP policy does not cover costs of hotels and other additional living expenses following a flood, while some private policies do. Coverage under the basement provisions of the MPPP policy is less broad than in some private policies. Specifically, the NFIP includes sunken rooms or portion of room in the definition of *basement* (where it provides limited coverage), while some private policies do not. Private policies will usually cover condominium association assessments on a condominium unit owner to cover the condominium association's deductible or the uninsured losses due to the lack of adequate insurance coverage, while the MPPP policy will not.

Finally, the private policies reviewed provide broader coverage than the MPPP policy for detached garages and other detached structures. First, the MPPP policy covers only detached garages, while the private policies cover other detached structures as well. Second, the MPPP policy limits coverage to 10 percent of the policy limit, and payments on detached garages count toward the policy limit. Private policies also limit payments to 10 percent of the policy limit, but some do not count the payments against the policy limit.

Turning to dimensions for which private policy coverage is not as broad as that provided by MPPP policies, the deductible on the MPPP policies is $500, whereas $750 is common in private policies. It should be noted, however, that policyholders can choose a deductible anywhere from $500 to $5,000 in the standard NFIP policy, so the deductible in private policies is at least consistent with the overall NFIP convention. In contrast to the MPPP policies,

---

[14] Because the analysis here applies to residential structures, we do not consider policies on structures with more than four units. The number of units in the structure is not an issue for provisions on replacement costs in MPPP policies written on individual condominium units.

[15] MPPP policies pay the actual cash value of the loss otherwise.

[16] For example, assume that a single-family, primary residence has a $50,000 mortgage and $50,000 in flood insurance and that the replacement value of the home is $150,000. If the replacement cost for the damage due to flood were $50,000, private policies would pay $50,000, but the MPPP policy would pay only the depreciated value (actual cash value) of the damaged property.

contents coverage is generally not available in lender-placed private flood insurance policies, because contents usually do not secure the loan and thus lenders do not have an insurable interest in them. This difference is not of much practical importance, however, because contents coverage is rarely force-placed, and thus contents coverage capabilities of MPPP policies are seldom used.

While the coverage for debris removal and loss avoidance measures (e.g., sandbags and labor) provided by some private policies are comparable to that provided by MPPP policies, the coverage provided by others is not as extensive. MPPP policies do not impose a sublimit on debris removal, while some private policies will cover only up to $1,000. The MPPP policy allows $1,000 in loss avoidance measures, while some of the private policies reviewed limit coverage to $500. Finally, at the time of our review, some private policies had lower limits on increased cost of compliance coverage than did the MPPP policy.[17] The private policies we reviewed were current as of early to mid-2005, and the limits on debris removal, loss avoidance measures, and cost of compliance may have increased in the interim. Verifying whether the limits have increased is a challenging task because rates and forms for some of the private insurers are filed separately in each state.

Policy Premiums

Private flood insurance policies are generally more expensive than the NFIP's standard flood insurance policy but substantially less expensive than the MPPP policy. As shown in Table 4.2, survey respondents reported premiums on private policies that range from $0.80 to $0.97 per $100 of coverage for homes in A flood zones.[18] A-zone rates for standard flood insurance policies are lower than rates on private policies, particularly for coverage above $50,000. The differences are more marked for homes in V zones.[19]

Private policies are less expensive than MPPP policies, with the difference particularly pronounced in A zones.[20] Lower prices could be one reason that lenders prefer private policies to MPPP policies (this issue will be explored in Chapter Five), but the higher prices of private policies relative to the standard flood insurance policy is almost certainly an important reason for the low proportion of private policies that remain in force for the entire one-year policy term.

---

[17] Increased cost of compliance coverage covers the costs of rebuilding a structure to more stringent building codes than were in place when the structure was originally built.

[18] In some cases, private insurer rates vary by state, but private insurers do not appear to have detailed state-based rating schedules. The private insurer rates in Table 4.2 reflect typical rates.

[19] The figures in Table 4.2 reflect rates that have not been adjusted to incorporate the increased estimates of flood risk post–Hurricane Katrina (which occurred in August 2005). The private rates were based on information collected between late 2004 and mid-2005. The NFIP rates reflect the 4.1-percent increase in May 2006 (FEMA, 2005), but they do not reflect changes in expected losses due to Hurricane Katrina (Thomas, 2006).

[20] One reason that lender-placed policies (either private or MPPP) might be more expensive than standard NFIP policies is that limited information is collected on the structure during the application process, and the rate must thus allow for the possibility that expected losses on the structure are high. Examination of the factors driving the differences between the standard NFIP, private, and MPPP rates, however, was beyond the scope of this study.

Table 4.2
Private and NFIP Premiums for Residential Structure Coverage

Policy	A Zones ($ per $100 of coverage)	V Zones ($ per $100 of coverage)	Deductible ($)
Standard flood insurance policy			
Pre-FIRM structures[a]	0.76/0.40[c]	0.99/1.03[c]	1,000
Post-FIRM structures[b]	0.61/0.08[c]	0.79	500
Private policy	0.80–0.97	2.75–3.35	750 in A zones; 1,000 in V zones
MPPP policy	2.52/1.26[c]	3.00/3.92[c]	500

SOURCE: Prices for private policies based on stakeholder interviews. Prices for the standard flood insurance policy and the MPPP policy were effective as of May 1, 2006 (NFIP, ongoing).

[a] For single-family homes with no basement or enclosure.

[b] For single-family homes with no basement or enclosure with lowest living floor one foot above the BFE.

[c] The first number is the premium rate for the first $50,000 of coverage, the second is the rate for additional coverage up to $250,000.

Summary

To place flood insurance that meets the standards of the MPR, lenders must buy policies with adequate coverage limits and use policies that are as broad as those offered by the NFIP. Our findings suggest that lenders typically place coverage with limits that meet or exceed the coverage requirements of the MPR. Our findings also suggest that the private policies cover some risks that MPPP policies do not (e.g., mudslides). Private policies also offer a number of features valuable to lenders that MPPP policies do not, including backdating, gap policies, and automatic coverage.

While the private policies reviewed meet or exceed MPPP policies in terms of many of the losses covered, some did not meet or exceed MPPP policies in a few dimensions. Thus, strictly speaking, some private policies do not appear to satisfy the requirements of the MPR. However, two important caveats are warranted. First, it is very difficult to assemble a complete picture of the coverage details of private policies, because insurers are reluctant to disclose what they often consider proprietary information and because policy terms can vary across the 50 states. Insurers may have updated some of the terms and conditions of their policies since we did our review. In particular, the insurers reporting only a $15,000 or $20,000 limit on increased cost of compliance coverage may have increased this limit, at least in some states. A second caveat is that some of the shortcomings of private policies may not be particularly significant; however, it is up to policymakers to make such an assessment. In any case, our analysis identifies a few provisions of private policies that deserve attention when evaluating whether the private policies satisfy the MPR.

CHAPTER FIVE

Stakeholder Perceptions of the Advantages of the Private Market

As discussed in previous chapters, lenders almost always choose to force-place policies through the private market rather than the NFIP's MPPP, and this chapter explores why. During the stakeholder interviews, we asked respondents what the advantages were of private policies over MPPP policies.[1] This chapter summarizes the answers.

As shown in Table 5.1, the ability to backdate private policies was the most widely cited advantage of private policies over NFIP policies. All six lenders interviewed praised backdating as did three of five insurers and trackers.[2] The NFIP grants a 30-day grace period to renew policies, but, even if trackers identify nonrenewals as soon as the policy expires, the 45-day waiting period required before a flood insurance policy can be force-placed exposes lenders to risk. Lenders value the private policies because they eliminate this risk. Further underscoring the importance of eliminating windows in which loans are uninsured, automatic coverage was also one of the most frequently cited advantages of private policies (see Chapter Three for a discussion of automatic coverage). NFIP policies offer neither backdating nor automatic coverage.

Lenders frequently praised private insurers for providing customer friendly service and products and being responsive to the needs of the private sector. The gap policies developed by private insurers have filled an important lender need, highlighting the unavailability of gap policies from the NFIP. Some of the lenders and trackers interviewed for the study expressed frustration with the complexity of the NFIP, NFIP staff turnover, and difficulty of finding NFIP staff who have a detailed understanding of the program.[3]

Many of the remaining advantages raised by survey participants pertain to the ease of using private policies to force-place insurance. The MPPP requires a homeowner signature before a policy can be cancelled (NFIP, ongoing, p. MPPP-6), whereas as a signature is not required to cancel a lender-placed private policy. Given the high percentage of lender-placed policies that are then cancelled sometime during the policy term, foregoing a signature on cancellation relieves lenders of substantial burden and cost. Again in contrast to the MPPP,

---

[1] Lenders can also force-place policies using the NFIP's standard flood insurance policy, but the detailed information required by the standard flood insurance policy (see Chapter Four) makes this approach impractical.

[2] We did not always prompt survey respondents about the features of the private policies that are attractive to lenders. Thus, even though two of the five insurers and trackers did not mention backdating, it should not be inferred that they thought backdating was unimportant.

[3] The respondents raising these concerns were referring to staff in FEMA's NFIP program. They were not referring to staff that run the flood insurance programs at WYO companies.

Table 5.1
Perceived Advantages of Private Flood Insurance Policies Over MPPP Policies

Advantage of Private Policies Relative to MPPP Policies	Number of Respondents Citing Advantage	
	Lenders (out of 6)	Trackers and Insurers (out of 5)
Ability to backdate policies	6	3
Automatic coverage	2	3
Customer friendly and good service	4	1
Requires less information on property to write the policy	3	1
Cheaper	2	1
Good claims adjustment and processing	2	1
Letter cycle not required for renewal	1	1
Signature not required to cancel policy	1	1
Cover additional living expenses	1	1
Available outside NFIP communities	1	1
Private insurers know how to process lender data	1	0
Efficiency of using same insurer as for other risks	1	0

a letter cycle is not required to renew a lender-placed policy (at least according to some lenders), reducing the burden on lenders. One lender commented that private insurers have invested in computer systems that can process lender databases, which provides a much quicker way to issue policies than is currently available for MPPP policies. Private insurers also have an advantage over the MPPP because they already write force-placed policies for other hazards. Lenders save costs by using one insurer for all of their insurance needs rather than maintaining relationships with multiple insurers. Finally, half of the lenders interviewed believed that private policies require less information to write than MPPP policies. However, this belief is inaccurate. As discussed in Chapter Three, the NFIP standard flood insurance policy requires considerably more information to write than private policies, but the information requirements for MPPP policies are roughly comparable to private policies.

Stakeholders found several additional features of private policies preferable to the policy offered by the MPPP. Two of the six lenders and one of the five trackers and insurers found the lower prices of private policies attractive.[4] A few survey respondents also pointed to the availability of additional living expenses (e.g., costs of hotels while the home is uninhabitable) and the ability to write policies in communities that do not participate in the NFIP as advantages of private policies.

[4] It is not surprising that only a minority of lenders mentioned price. Borrowers, not lenders, pay for the insurance, although higher prices presumably impact lenders to the extent that they reduce borrowers' ability to repay loans.

Overall, the private sector expressed strong preferences for private policies over the MPPP policies offered by the NFIP. Just considering the convenience of using the same insurer for force-placing flood policies as for other risks, MPPP policies would likely need to be considerably better than private policies for the lenders and trackers to consider using them. And as indicated in the interviews, private policies have advantages in many other dimensions. Lenders will likely continue to use private insurers to force-place policies absent considerable changes in MPPP policies and procedures or substantial deterioration in the service offered by or financial strength of private insurers.

CHAPTER SIX

Conclusions

This report attempts (1) to provide better estimates of the number of flood insurance policies underwritten by private insurers, (2) to compare the policies offered by the private sector with those offered by the NFIP, and (3) to characterize stakeholder perceptions of the private market. In this concluding chapter, we review the key findings of the study and discuss their policy implications.

Magnitude of the Private Residential Flood Insurance Market

Private insurance plays a key role in lender procedures to comply with the NFIP's MPR. Lenders almost exclusively choose to force-place flood insurance on residential properties using private policies rather than policies available from the NFIP.

Although the interest of private insurers in selling residential policies in the voluntary market appears to be growing, this market appears to remain small, so private involvement in the residential market is predominantly through compliance with the MPR. Private insurers play a much more substantial role in insuring commercial structures, and, in contrast to residential structures, private insurers appear to provide insurance on commercial structures primarily through the voluntary market rather than via lender-placed policies.

Estimates developed here on the number of primary lender–placed policies on residential structures are consistent with previous estimates. Our findings suggest that roughly 130,000 to 190,000 primary policies are in place at any one time. While the sample size on which the findings are based is not large, the consistency of estimates using data from different categories of stakeholders and the consistency of the findings with a preexisting estimate increase confidence in the findings. Private insurers also appear to write a sizable number of gap policies, although data on gap policies are sketchy. Including gap policies may increase the number of private policies to between 180,000 and 260,000. Gap policies do not increase the total number of households covered by flood insurance, but rather increase the dollar amount of flood coverage in place.

The number of private policies is not large compared with the 5.0 million residential policies written by the NFIP. Including this relatively small number of private policies thus does not result in a large increase in estimates of the proportion of structures covered by flood insurance (the market penetration rate).[1] However, the number of policies currently in place is not the only measure of the importance of the private insurers in implementing the MPR. First, few lender-placed policies remain in effect for the one-year policy term, with the implication that many more policies are issued per year than the number of policies currently in place indicates. Thus, private policies insure far more structures at some point during the year than the number of policies in place at a point in time indicates.

Second, the automatic coverage endorsement that many lenders purchase increases the number of homes effectively insured beyond the number of policies in place. With the automatic coverage endorsement, all homes in the lender's portfolio subject to the MPR are, in effect, covered for losses. Previous estimates of compliance with the MPR have factored in estimates only of the number of private residential policies. Compliance would be higher if it included all loans covered by automatic coverage endorsements. However, further work is needed to understand the magnitude of this effect. Better information is needed on the proportion of properties covered by the automatic coverage endorsement, and data on how often automatic coverage endorsements are triggered (for example, during Hurricane Katrina) would be useful.

Comparison of Private and NFIP Policies

Private policies used to satisfy the MPR must meet or exceed coverage offered by NFIP policies. We found that the private policies that lenders force-place on residential properties meet or exceed MPR requirements for the amount of coverage and covered some risks that the NFIP policy does not (e.g., mudslides). We also found that private policies meet or exceed NFIP policies in terms of many of the losses covered, but, in a few dimensions, such as coverage limits for debris removal or increased cost of compliance coverage, private policies were not as comprehensive as NFIP policies.

While the coverage in private policies meets or exceeds the coverage offered by NFIP policies in many areas, the failure to meet or exceed NFIP provisions in some dimensions raises the possibility that private policies do not comply with MPR requirements. It is up to policymakers to assess whether these differences are significant. Some of the private policies may have been updated since the date we obtained the policies (early to mid-2005), and additional research is also warranted on the extent to which coverage in these dimensions has improved over time.

Perceptions of the Advantages of the Private Market

Private policies offer features that are attractive to lenders that NFIP policies do not. The stakeholders interviewed highlighted the ability to backdate private policies to the start of

---

[1]   Dixon, Clancy, et al. (2006, p. 15) estimated that 1.76 million of the 3.57 million single-family homes in SFHAs carry policies from the NFIP (49 percent). If private lender–placed policies increase the number of single-family homes insured by 160,000, the market penetration rate for flood insurance (including both NFIP and non-NFIP policies) would rise to 54 percent.

the letter cycle and the automatic coverage endorsement. They also praised the service that private insurers provided and the ease of using their products. Lenders appear very satisfied with the products and services that private insurers provided and expressed no interest in using the MPPP to force-place policies. The MPPP program would need to change in fundamental ways to attract private lenders.

This study could not examine perceptions of private insurers from the perspective of policyholders. Indirect indications from lenders, who were satisfied with the claims process, suggest that disputes in the claims process do not regularly arise. Further research is needed, however, to more fully understand how homeowner satisfaction with claims adjustment for lender-placed policies compares with satisfaction with the adjustment of NFIP claims.

Role of Private Insurers

Congress established the NFIP in 1968 in part due to the ongoing unavailability of private flood insurance. Over the years, however, a deepening partnership between the federal government and the private insurance industry has emerged. The main role the private insurance industry plays in providing flood insurance to residential structures is selling and servicing NFIP policies. However, private insurers underwrite flood insurance in a limited, but important, niche. In doing so, they increase the number of homes protected by flood insurance, developing innovative policy provisions that respond to lender and borrower needs and providing streamlined services that reduce the costs lenders incur in complying with the MPR.

References

Bender, Bruce, "Alternatives to the NFIP: What Other Choices Are There?" paper presented at the National Flood Conference, Philadelphia, Pa., May 9, 2006.

Carroll, Stephen J., Tom LaTourrette, Brian G. Chow, Gregory S. Jones, and Craig Martin, *Distribution of Losses from Large Terrorist Attacks Under the Terrorism Risk Insurance Act*, Santa Monica, Calif.: RAND Corporation, MG-427-CTRMP, 2005. As of March 2, 2007:
http://www.rand.org/pubs/monographs/MG427/

Chubb Corporation, "New Flood Insurance Policy Provides Up to $15 Million in Limits," press release, Warren, N.J., April 3, 2006. As of May 6, 2006:
http://www.chubb.com/corporate/chubb4991.html

Dixon, Lloyd, John Arlington, Stephen Carroll, Darius Lakdawalla, Robert Reville, and David Adamson, *Issues and Options for Government Intervention in the Market for Terrorism Insurance*, Santa Monica, Calif.: RAND Corporation, OP-135-ICJ, 2004. As of March 2, 2007:
http://www.rand.org/pubs/occasional_papers/OP135/

Dixon, Lloyd, Noreen Clancy, Seth A. Seabury, and Adrian Overton, *The National Flood Insurance Program's Market Penetration Rate: Estimates and Policy Implications*, Santa Monica, Calif.: RAND Corporation, TR-300-FEMA, 2006. As of March 2, 2007:
http://www.rand.org/pubs/technical_reports/TR300/

Dixon, Lloyd, and Rachel Kaganoff Stern, *Compensation for Losses from the 9/11 Attacks*, Santa Monica, Calif.: RAND Corporation, MG-264-ICJ, 2004. As of March 2, 2007:
http://www.rand.org/pubs/monographs/MG264/

FEMA—*see* U.S. Federal Emergency Management Agency.

Mortgage Bankers Association, "Top 300 Single-Family Residential (1 to 4 Unit) Mortgage Lenders: 2003 Home Purchase Originations Ranked by Dollar Volume," 2005.

National Flood Insurance Program, "Policies in Force (PIF): Rolling 12 Months," undated Web page. As of September 29, 2006:
http://bsa.nfipstat.com/reports/pifhist.htm

———, *Flood Insurance Manual*, Washington, D.C.: NFIP, ongoing (latest version effective May 1, 2007). As of March 2, 2007:
http://www.fema.gov/business/nfip/manual.shtm

NFIP—*see* National Flood Insurance Program.

Scoville, Tim, systems development director, National Flood Insurance Program, personal communication based on data from W2RMMPPP report, July 31, 2006, Lanham, Md.

Thomas, David, "Giving Growth a Boost," *Watermark*, No. 1, 2004, pp. 1, 4–5. As of March 1, 2007:
http://www.fema.gov/pdf/nfip/wm2004_1.pdf

———, U.S. Federal Emergency Management Agency, National Flood Insurance Program, personal communication, November 11, 2006, Washington, D.C.

Tobin, Richard J., and Corinne Calfee, *The National Flood Insurance Program's Mandatory Purchase Requirement: Policies, Processes, and Stakeholders*, Washington, D.C.: American Institutes for Research, 2005.

U.S. Census Bureau, *Current Housing Reports: H-150, American Housing Survey for the United States in 2005*, Washington, D.C.: U.S. Department of Commerce, Bureau of the Census, August 2006. As of August 29, 2006:
http://www.census.gov/prod/2006pubs/h150-05.pdf

U.S. Federal Emergency Management Agency, "National Flood Insurance Program: Participating Insurance Companies," undated Web page. As of January 17, 2007:
http://www.fema.gov/nfipInsurance/companies.jsp

———, *Mandatory Purchase of Flood Insurance Guidelines*, Washington, D.C.: FEMA, 1999.

———, *National Flood Insurance Program: Program Description*, Washington, D.C.: FEMA, August 1, 2002. As of March 2, 2007:
http://www.fema.gov/library/viewRecord.do?id=1480

———, "May 1, 2006, Program Changes," memorandum from David I. Maurstad, acting director of FEMA Mitigation Division to write-your-own principal coordinators and NFIP servicing agents, Washington, D.C., November 29, 2005. As of March 2, 2007:
http://na.iiaa.org/TFT/TFTLinks/Flood4.4.06/w-05083.pdf